AMERICAN MOMENTS

SCENES FROM AMERICAN HISTORY

Robert Burleigh   ILLUSTRATED BY **Bruce Strachan**

Henry Holt and Company • New York

Martin Luther King, Jr., with his young daughter Yolanda

AUTHOR'S NOTE

Of the numerous significant moments that make up our country's story, those featured in this book constitute a cross-section intended to represent the many facets of American life. Any observer could easily select other events equally important to the America of yesterday and today.

The facts—dates, events, people, and places—are true. But to *feel* the American story, we often need more than "the facts." Therefore I have tried to re-create some of the thoughts and emotions those involved *might* have experienced. I hope this will help evoke the real spirit of these particular episodes in American history.

An endnote is included for each moment at the back of the book. These notes, though brief, serve to broaden the context, to give further information, or in a few cases to answer a question that the treatment of the moment may have raised. However they are used, they remain an important part of the total book.

Contents

Thanksgiving Feast

OCTOBER 1621

THE AUTUMN SUN SPARKLES as men, women, and children bustle about. Some people set pudding pots on rough tree-stump tables. Others bring corn in large wooden bowls or cook meat over hot coals.

Squanto passes Priscilla and laughs. "And what is your work, Priscilla Mullins?" She is taking care of a friend's baby, ten-month-old Peregrine White, and rocking the wide-eyed infant in her arms.

Priscilla looks up with a start. On the high hill to the west, a band of Indians approaches in single file. But Squanto laughs again. "It's only Chief Massasoit and his hunters, with five more deer for our very special dinner."

The visitors come closer, down the narrow path to the single street. Then Priscilla does something strange. She holds tiny Peregrine way up over her head for everyone to see. *Look, our first-born Pilgrim child!* For a moment this boy-child seems like a sign that says: *We came through the cruel winter. We planted and harvested. And now we are on the other side. We will survive.*

Captain Myles Standish, decked out in his best white collar, waves his arm in the air, followed everywhere by loud cheers. *Welcome one and all. Let the feasting and the games begin!*

{7}

IN CONGRESS, JULY 4, 1776.
mous Declaration of the thirteen united States of America,
When in the Course of human events, it becomes necessary for one people to dissolve the political bands which have connected them with another, and to

Presenting the Declaration of Independence

JULY 1776

"GENTLEMEN, THE DECLARATION, PLEASE."

The room goes completely quiet, as a group of men approach the speaker. In the lead, his red hair blazing, is the main author—Thomas Jefferson. Beside him stands bespectacled Benjamin Franklin, an old man but with a still-boyish twinkle in his eye. They glance sideways at each other, the young revolutionary and the aging patriot. *Is it possible? Is it really happening? A new country?* On the other side of Jefferson, John Adams waits silently.

Jefferson places a sheaf of papers on the table. John Hancock gazes down. For a moment, the only sound is the soft crinkle of paper in his hands. He reads briefly to himself, then out loud:

We hold these truths to be self-evident, that all men are created equal, that they are endowed by their Creator with certain unalienable Rights, that among these are Life, Liberty, and the pursuit of Happiness. . . .

From the back of the room, many voices rise—"Hear! Hear! Hear!"

George Washington Crosses the Delaware

December 25, 1776

A RAW, WET NIGHT. General George Washington stares into the dark water before him, as the northeast wind whips into his face. The Revolutionary War, the war for American independence, has been going badly. *Will tonight be different?* Men gather in the rear. One whispers the night's password: *Liberty or Death.*

The general raises his arm. The boats begin to fill with soldiers. Some men are shoeless, with rags wrapped around their feet. Next, horses and cannons are brought aboard. Silently, others push the boats into the churning river.

Ice chunks clack against the dipping oars. A needle-like sleet begins to fall. The general's boat tips sideways but keeps its balance. Time stands still. Then suddenly, the underside of the first boat scrapes over the stones of the far shore. Washington steps out into ankle-deep water.

Quiet if you can! The men unload as their clothes freeze like cold armor to their bodies. Trenton is nine miles ahead. Is it a march toward victory or defeat? No one knows for sure. But—*forward!*

Lewis and Clark Reach the Pacific

JANUARY 8, 1806

A BRISK WIND RISES. Seagulls squawk overhead. Unseen surf washes up somewhere close at hand. A small band, with buckskin-clad William Clark in the lead, pushes through a tangle of brush and makes its way cautiously around a rocky hill.

There it is! Meriwether Lewis's dog, Seaman, barks and races forward while the others stand and stare. Sacagawea turns her small child toward the white breakers and says quietly, "Great waters. See?" York cheers. Lewis, the expedition's co-leader, points to the shore where a huge whale skeleton lies. Lewis then takes out a small notebook and begins to sketch. More notes for President Jefferson.

Clark pauses. He has already seen the Pacific, but each view thrills him. He remembers the more than two-thousand-mile journey past Indian tribes, down rivers, and over snow-capped mountains, the journey that led his little corps of explorers to this place. *Was it a dream, or did we come this far?* He watches the sun setting with a cold orange glow above the distant horizon. *Yes. We made it.*

Harriet Tubman and the Underground Railroad
OCTOBER 1851

THE WEARY, RAGGEDLY DRESSED men and women duck down and freeze in their tracks, listening as nearby voices rise and become clearer: "This here's the way, boys. We'll catch them runaway slaves. Come on." Horses' hooves clatter past and, echoing faintly, fade in the stillness of the night.

Finally, one of the men in the huddled group turns around. "Miss Harriet," he says in a shivering voice, "I'm not going on. We're lost. I'm goin' back."

The woman called Miss Harriet stares hard at the frightened man. Her eyes blaze with a steely determination. "Mister," she answers, "you heading back will outright ruin our escape plan. You've got just two choices now: to come with us—or die.

"Besides," Harriet Tubman continues, "we're not lost. See that star?" Pointing toward a distant twinkle in the sky, she says, "It's the North Star we're following. And it leads to freedom. So, all together, everyone. Let's up and get gone."

The Assassination of Abraham Lincoln

APRIL 14, 1865

WASHINGTON, D.C. Good Friday evening at Ford's Theatre. Abraham Lincoln shifts back and forth in his rocking chair. He looks down on the play in progress. It is act three. Behind him, at the rear of the box, the door is closed.

The play is silly, and President Lincoln's thoughts drift to other things. He sits basking in the warm glow of the standing ovation he received when he arrived at the theater. In his mind, he still hears the strains of the orchestra playing "Hail to the Chief." He rocks a little. The door behind him opens just a crack.

The front of the box is decorated with American flags. The president thinks of the war just concluded. The Union has been preserved, but so many have died. For a moment, Mrs. Lincoln puts her hand on her husband's arm. Behind them, through the narrow crack in the door, an eye—unfriendly—peers out of the darkness.

It is 10:30 P.M. For the most part, the nation sleeps. The play goes on. History waits. Then suddenly a shot rings out—and the president slumps forward.

Susan B. Anthony Demands Her Rights

JUNE 17, 1873

THE UNITED STATES COURTHOUSE in Canandaigua, New York. The judge, bristling with barely contained anger, raps his gavel. "The prisoner will stand up. This is the sentence of the court: You must pay a fine of one hundred dollars and the cost of prosecution."

The prisoner stands. Till now, she has not been allowed to speak. Why? *Because she is a woman!* She pauses. What shall Susan B. Anthony say? That she had a right, as an American citizen, to vote—as she attempted to vote—in the election of 1872? That she has crossed the country many times arguing (sometimes against the jeers of violent crowds) for women's rights? That she will never stop? That failure is impossible?

She stares through her thin-rimmed glasses. Her red shawl is draped, as always, over her shoulders. "May it please Your Honor," she says slowly but forcefully, "I will never pay a dollar of your unjust penalty. . . . And I shall continue to urge all women to the practical recognition of the old Revolutionary maxim: 'Resistance to tyranny is obedience to God.'"

Crazy Horse and Custer's Last Stand

JUNE 25, 1876

HOT SUN BURNS DOWN. The Sioux warriors splash across the Little Bighorn River in a rush of shouting voices and neighing horses. Somewhere on the other side of the hill are the soldiers of Lt. Colonel George Armstrong Custer—Long Hair—whose troops would steal the Indian lands and destroy their villages.

Crazy Horse halts and raises his arm. A single hawk feather juts from his braided locks. A painted lightning bolt zigzags down his cheek. *Is this the day?*

He remembers the sun-dance vision of the great spirit leader Sitting Bull. Did not Sitting Bull see many white soldiers and their horses falling upside down from the sky to their deaths? *Yes, today is a good day to fight! A good day to die!*

The plan: to descend on Long Hair and his unsuspecting troops before they can flee. Crazy Horse raises his arm again and lets out the war cry: "Hoka Hey, Hoka Hey!" Then, digging his heels into his pony's sides and fixing his gaze on the hill's crest, he gallops ahead.

An Immigrant Arrives at Ellis Island

SEPTEMBER 13, 1893

THE SS *Rhynland*, FILLED WITH IMMIGRANTS from Europe, churns through the choppy waters of New York Harbor. Ahead, a small island with many buildings lies in the river mouth.

Horns sound. Seagulls drift and swoop. Voices call out in many languages. Look! Passengers hurry to the railing and point, so many people that the ship seems to lurch dangerously.

"Quick, Father, pick me up." Five-year-old Israel Baline is lifted into his father's arms. Across the water, a huge statue looms against distant tall buildings. Little Israel sees a gigantic female figure holding a bronze torch high in the air.

"It's the torch of freedom," his father says, pointing and waving with the rest.

"What will we do here?" the boy asks.

"I'm not sure," Israel's father answers. "When you grow up, though, who knows? This is America. Much is possible." But Israel isn't listening anymore. He is craning his neck to get one last look at the beautiful lady rising out of the sea as the ship moves on.

The Wright Brothers' First Flight

December 17, 1903

KITTY HAWK, NORTH CAROLINA. The cold wind bites into Orville's outstretched hands as he lies flat and looks ahead. The *Flyer* teeters on the long wooden track the two Wright brothers like to call the "Grand Junction." The plane's small engine rattles against the sound of the nearby waves.

"Ready now, and let it go!" Orville grips the throttle as brother Wilbur runs alongside, supporting one of the wings. The plane, still on the track, moves slowly and awkwardly ahead. Then faster and faster. Wilbur lets go and watches. The plane rocks from side to side.

The *Flyer* chugs into the air! It barely leaves the ground (not by much—but enough). Wilbur waves wildly as Orville struggles to steady the wind-blown wings. Three seconds, four seconds, five, six, seven...

And then, dipping to one side, the plane bounces back to earth. But who cares? The *Flyer* was airborne for twelve full seconds and 120 feet! The brothers know the truth: For the first time in human history, a heavier-than-air machine has successfully headed for the skies.

Houdini Escapes Again
November 6, 1916

HANGING BY HIS HEELS, his body bound so tightly the blood stabs at his head, Houdini glances down. Far below him, he sees a whirling kaleidoscope of hats, upturned faces, stalled tramcars, and horse-drawn carriages hemmed in by the packed Pittsburgh crowd that numbers over 10,000.

His shoulders strain against the leather "shirt" that has held lunatics and murderers. He feels the rough edge of the straitjacket cutting into his neck. The spectators watch, mouths open, ready to gasp.

Houdini flips and spins like a trapped creature. *Never. No chains can keep me bound.* He rocks and careens into a near-standing position, parallel to the rope he dangles from. He hurts, twisting in a thousand wild directions.

Suddenly, one arm pokes out from his straitjacket prison. A sea of voices rises like a great wave from below. A second arm flaps out. Houdini thrusts his knees, shimmies, rolls, kicks. The straitjacket slips down over his head and into one of his waiting hands. He holds it out a moment, then lets it fall earthward like a useless wing. He spreads his arms in triumph.

Houdini, Houdini. Free again!

Georgia O'Keeffe Paints a Picture

SUMMER 1929

IN THE HOT NEW MEXICO SUN, a lone hiker walks past a long line of juniper trees. It is a landscape pockmarked with wind-sculpted rocks and sun-bleached bones.

Georgia O'Keeffe shades her eyes. She is already famous in New York. But here everything is unbelievably new. An unpainted world. A wonderful emptiness. Craggy peaks, silent sandstone hills, and cliffs whose colors shift each minute with the slow-rising sun. *Hurry. Hurry. Before it goes.*

She plants her wide umbrella in a steady place. She unfolds her easel. A single hawk soars high against the cloudless blue. Georgia O'Keeffe takes up her brush. *The world is big, far beyond my understanding.* In the distance, there is a shimmery wave of violet and purple light. Can she capture this moment? Before it fades? She isn't sure. But now the brush softly swishes over the empty canvas, and the work begins.

Franklin Roosevelt's Fireside Chat

MARCH 12, 1933

IT IS 10 P.M. IN THE WHITE HOUSE. The new president wheels himself to the edge of the desk. He has been in office only one week, but tonight Franklin Delano Roosevelt will speak to a country that is very afraid. Millions of people are out of work. Millions more fear losing their jobs. Some have lost their life savings. Now the people listen, gathered around radios in forty-eight states.

Does the president feel the nation's despair because he himself despaired once, too? His thoughts return to the dark days when polio first left him crippled, bound for life to heavy leg braces and a clumsy chair. Yet fortified by his own will and Eleanor's strength, he survived. He survived to be here tonight—to bring what? Courage? Hope? A recovery plan?

Franklin Roosevelt hears himself introduced: "The president wants to come into your home and sit at your fireside for a little fireside chat." Yes, it will be like that. One-to-one. As if he were speaking to a friend in the next room. The president leans forward. His voice is clear, calm, confident:

We start tomorrow. . . . Let us unite in banishing fear. . . . Together we cannot fail. . . .

Raising the Flag on Iwo Jima

February 23, 1945

A cautious line of forty U.S. Marines moves up the side of an extinct volcano called Mount Suribachi. Behind the men are four days of intense fighting. The Iwo Jima island is only an eight-square-mile chunk of black volcanic ash and barren rock. But the Japanese soldiers, hunkered down in caves and tunnels, will fight to the death.

The marines zigzag upward, listening for gunfire that never comes. At the upper ridge, the men stumble upon a length of old pipe, which they use as a pole to raise a small flag. From down below, and even from the nearby ships at sea, cheers and whistles pierce the morning air. The Americans have captured the highest point on the island!

Someone brings an even larger flag. Six men lean and haul and thrust as the second flag rises, fluttering in the wind. A photographer snaps a picture. *Click.*

Still, World War II is far from over. And three of the flag raisers will not leave this island alive. The flag is a symbol of hope, of distant victory, of peace.

Rosa Parks Starts a Boycott
DECEMBER 1, 1955

MONTGOMERY, ALABAMA. She sits quietly, lost in the gentle rumble of the motor. Then the bus driver calls back to her and three others. The words are harsh and staccato: "You four, move. Empty those seats." She is sitting in a seat that, if white people are standing, she must give up. But why? Hasn't she paid her fare?

The driver growls his command a second time. The other three African-Americans stand up, walk to the rear. But not Rosa Parks. Something—she isn't sure what—keeps her here. In this seat.

A tiny voice inside her asks if she is too tired to stand and move. *No, not tired like that,* she answers the voice. *The only tired I am is tired of giving in.*

A minute passes. Everyone is silent. The driver hovers above her now, red-faced, a small mole near his angry mouth. His lips curl into a threat: "I'm going to have you arrested."

Rosa Parks stares straight ahead. "You may do that" is all she says softly. "You may do that."

Ellington and Armstrong—Together at Last

APRIL 3, 1961

THE PIANO SOUNDS LIGHTLY and the singer waits. In a New York City recording studio, Duke Ellington bends over the keys. Louis "Satchmo" Armstrong leans toward the microphone.

Two great rivers of jazz, recording together for the first and only time. The River of Duke—smooth-flowing, calm-surfaced, clear—and the River of Satchmo—bursting forth, bubbly with life, pressing against the banks. *One, two—one, two, three, four. . .*

Duke smiles and nods, fingers feathering the keys. The opening song is "Duke's Place," an Ellington composition. Satchmo's gravelly voice breaks into the *tap-tap-tap* of the blues piano. Now Duke solos, backed by bass and drum. Other instruments join in. The high-pitched swirl of a clarinet. The playful flicker of a trumpet. The edgy wail of a trombone. Yes, it *is* Duke's place.

So sing it again, Satchmo. Let it swing!

Neil Armstrong Steps on the Moon!

July 20, 1969

THE LANDING CRAFT'S SPIDERY LEGS hover and slowly descend above craters and threatening boulders. Finally the legs touch, shuddering and vibrating but holding firm. The moon! After more than 220,000 miles (four days from Earth), "The Eagle has landed."

A narrow hatch opens, and an astronaut emerges. He moves awkwardly in his bulky spacesuit. He eases himself carefully, step by step, down the ten-foot ladder. He sees in every direction the bleak yet oddly beautiful emptiness of the untouched moon. Standing at last on the module's wide footpad, he pauses to study the fine-grained powdery surface.

The astronaut lowers his foot and creates the first human footprint on the moon. (It looks like the mark a heavy boot might leave in snow.) He speaks, his distant voice crackling as it sounds back to the millions of watchers and listeners:

That's one small step for man, one giant leap for mankind.

There is no other sound. Then Neil Armstrong, leaning slightly forward to keep his balance, walks slowly into a new world.

We Remember 9/11

OCTOBER 2001

SOMEWHERE ELSE, the trees are changing to a lustrous gold. Somewhere else, corn is hauled into a barn, footballs spiral in the clear air, a fall breeze that hints of winter rides down over the rivers. Somewhere else.

But here they simply stand and look. Who are they? People of many colors. Mothers and fathers. Children. Girls and boys and wrinkled old men. Dreamers. Thinkers. Doers. Americans all.

They stand behind the wooden barrier. The rubble, still smoking in places, rises five stories high. A mountain of destroyed steel and glass and stone. A place called Ground Zero.

They remember, too. They remember tall buildings that soared toward the clouds. They remember the courage. They remember the firefighters, racing up stairs that too soon came crashing down. They remember the dead. They remember names: Burke, Fox, Gonzales, Petrocelli, Yuen.

October 2001. Quietly, they look and remember. They hold softly flickering candles. *No*, they say to themselves, *we will never forget.*

Endnotes

THANKSGIVING FEAST

The Pilgrims had good reason to pause and rejoice. Their first winter in the New World was 1620–21. During those cold, bitter months, half of their party of 102 men, women, and children had died. But this difficult time had been followed by a summer of fruitful planting and an abundant autumn harvest.

Priscilla Mullins, then just a young woman, lived to be a mother herself. And what about little Peregrine White (whose first name means Pilgrim in Latin)? He went on to live to the ripe old age of eighty-four!

The exact date of the first Thanksgiving is not known. We do know that Governor William Bradford arranged a harvest festival in the autumn of 1621 and that Native People attended the three-day festival. Colonial Americans continued to celebrate a thanksgiving day, but it was not made a formal holiday until 1863, when President Abraham Lincoln proclaimed one, to be held the last Thursday of each November. This was changed slightly in 1941, when Congress made Thanksgiving Day the fourth Thursday of November.

PRESENTING THE DECLARATION OF INDEPENDENCE

The American Declaration of Independence was approved and adopted by the Second Continental Congress in Philadelphia on July 4, 1776. The approval came, however, only after a long period of writing, debate, and rewriting. Thomas Jefferson, the main author, worked on the Declaration for more than two weeks. Jefferson's version was amended in both small and major ways. (One major change was that his criticism of the slave trade was eliminated in the final version.)

Benjamin Franklin advised and aided in the writing of the document. So did others, including John Adams, who would become the second president of the United States. (Jefferson himself would become the third president.) Franklin, seventy years old in 1776, was at that time the most famous American in the world, widely known and much praised as an inventor, a scientist, an author, and a diplomat.

GEORGE WASHINGTON CROSSES THE DELAWARE

The Continental Army's bold crossing of the Delaware River, and their surprise attack at Trenton, New Jersey, changed the course of the American Revolution (1775–83). Until then, George Washington's army had suffered defeats and been forced to retreat several times. The colonists' struggle for independence from Great Britain seemed almost doomed.

The victory at Trenton (and one week later, at Princeton) buoyed American hopes and brought more volunteer soldiers into the fighting. One historian has written: "Seldom in history has such a small battle had a more profound effect on the outcome of a war."

LEWIS AND CLARK REACH THE PACIFIC

The "voyage of discovery" led by Meriwether Lewis and William Clark is one of the great exploratory expeditions in human history. From St. Louis to the Pacific Ocean and back, the journey took about two and a half years and covered more than 7,000 miles—by canoe, on horseback, and on foot. The corps of travelers consisted of around forty people in all. And strange as it seems, only one member died during that time.

The travelers were helped on the way by several Native American tribes. Sacagawea (a young Shoshone woman traveling with her infant son, nicknamed Pomp) aided the group by acting as an interpreter. York, an African-American slave, was a full member of the expedition.

Actually, Lewis, Clark, and just a few others saw the Pacific for the first time on November 7, 1805. (Clark's diary for that day records it: "Ocean in view. O! The joy!") But Sacagawea wanted to see the "great waters," too. The explorers were camped a short distance inland, so she persuaded the leaders to take her to the coast about two months later.

HARRIET TUBMAN AND THE UNDERGROUND RAILROAD

Harriet Tubman's bravery and soldier-like discipline earned her the nickname of "the Moses of her people." An escaped slave herself, during the 1850s Tubman returned to the South nineteen times and led more than 300 slaves to freedom—without ever losing a "passenger" on the Underground Railroad. (She often carried a pistol for protection and to enforce discipline along the way.) Two people she led to freedom were her own parents. She also worked for the Union Army as a spy in the Civil War and still later for the women's suffrage movement.

Tubman's legendary escapes were carefully planned. She often began her flights on a Saturday night, because newspapers were not published on Sundays and thus news of the escape would get less publicity for more than twenty-four hours. At one time, there was a reward of $40,000 for her capture.

THE ASSASSINATION OF ABRAHAM LINCOLN

Abraham Lincoln's assassin, John Wilkes Booth, crept into the theater box and shot the president once in the head, mortally wounding him. Lincoln died the following morning, as a stunned nation heard the news. "Now," one of his advisors said, "he belongs to the ages."

Lincoln had guided the country through four long years of civil war, from 1861 to 1865. The slaves were free at last. The nation was united again. But Lincoln himself had become a weary, careworn man.

After the shooting, Booth escaped from the theater but

was discovered in hiding less than two weeks later and killed in a gun battle with his pursuers.

SUSAN B. ANTHONY DEMANDS HER RIGHTS

Susan B. Anthony, along with her close friend and co-reformer Elizabeth Cady Stanton, struggled energetically for more than fifty years to gain American women the right to vote. Anthony's attempt to vote in 1872—and the trial that followed—caused a national uproar.

Stanton was the philosophic guide and Anthony was the practical arm of a movement that included thousands of women (as well as many men) fighting for universal suffrage. The two women also campaigned for a woman's right to own property and her right to have guardianship over her children in case of divorce.

Anthony's last public words, uttered before her death in 1906, proved prophetic. "Failure is impossible," she proclaimed. Fourteen years later the Nineteenth Amendment (also known as the Anthony Amendment), giving women voting rights at last, was added to the U.S. Constitution.

CRAZY HORSE AND CUSTER'S LAST STAND

When it was over, it would be known as the Battle of the Little Bighorn or, more famously, as Custer's Last Stand. The Sioux, under Crazy Horse, killed 250 United States soldiers, including the overconfident Lt. Colonel George Armstrong Custer. Custer was called Long Hair by the Native People because he let his light-colored hair grow in long locks. Today, there is a national monument in southeastern Montana, where the battle took place.

The Sioux victory, however, didn't end the wars in the West. Eventually, Crazy Horse and Sitting Bull ceased fighting, and both died at the hands of American troops. Today, no one knows where Crazy Horse is buried. Still, one Oglala Sioux has written: "It does not matter where his body lies, for it is grass; but where his spirit is, it will be good to be."

An Immigrant Arrives at Ellis Island

Little Israel Baline was just one of millions of immigrants who, more than a hundred years ago, passed by the Statue of Liberty and disembarked at Ellis Island. At that time, Ellis Island was where newcomers from Europe to the United States first landed. From there they entered the country to begin their new lives.

Most immigrants worked very hard, and a few, like Israel Baline, even became famous. Of course, you don't know him by that name. But you may know the name he took when he became one of our most popular songwriters: Irving Berlin. And even if you don't recognize the name, you surely know many of his songs. One is "White Christmas." Another is—yes— "God Bless America"!

The Wright Brothers' First Flight

During the last decade of the nineteenth century, many people were trying to get an airplane off the ground. The Wright brothers were first to succeed (in 1903). But it took Wilbur and Orville Wright many years of scientific study and physical labor to build and test the *Flyer*. On that same historic December day, however, they made three more flights. The longest lasted almost one minute, and the plane traveled more than 800 feet.

Even after the brothers got their first plane airborne, many people still refused to believe it was possible. It was not until several years later that the United States government showed any interest in the new "flying machine." Soon, however, the Wrights' invention was recognized for what it was: one of the most important advances in science and technology in modern times.

Houdini Escapes Again

Houdini's spectacular escapes, including the Suspended Straitjacket Escape, the Manacled Bridge Jump, and the Milk Can Escape, drew thousands into the streets and theaters of America in the pre-television age. The same year that Houdini performed his Straitjacket Escape in Pittsburgh, he also attracted crowds of 20,000 spectators in Los Angeles and 50,000 in Baltimore with this daring feat.

Was it trickery? Perhaps. But Harry Houdini, who was born Ehrich Weiss in 1874 and died in 1926, also studied magic very carefully and was in excellent physical condition. Today his name still symbolizes mystery, skill, and the passion to be free.

Georgia O'Keeffe Paints a Picture

When Georgia O'Keeffe died in 1986 (at age ninety-eight) she was one of the most famous artists in the world. Known for her strongly independent spirit and her self-discipline, O'Keeffe decided at an early age to become a painter. (She did this even though there were few opportunities for women artists at that time.)

Before and during the 1920s, she lived in New York, where she was considered a pioneer of modern American art. Then, in 1929, a visit to New Mexico astonished her with that region's stark beauty. Her many rides and walks in the desert landscape became the basis for new subjects and a changing style.

The subjects of O'Keeffe's work varied over the years. She painted lyrical abstractions, cityscapes, large flowers, and scenes from the American Southwest. "If you are an artist," she once said, "you must keep the unknown always beyond you."

Franklin Roosevelt's Fireside Chat

Franklin Delano Roosevelt was the thirty-second president of the United States. Elected president four times, between 1932 and 1944, he led the nation during the Great Depression and during a large part of World War II. Many of his New Deal programs (such as Social Security) are still in place today. He often used his radio talks, called fireside chats, to communicate with the American people.

His wife, Eleanor Roosevelt, brought a new vigor and importance to the role of First Lady. For many years she spoke out on behalf of minorities and for human rights.

Mrs. Roosevelt was also influential in the founding of the United Nations.

Raising the Flag on Iwo Jima

The capture of Iwo Jima was an important step in the victory by the United States over Japan in World War II. Although the island was tiny, it had been used by the Japanese to launch air strikes against Allied forces. After the island's capture, U.S. fighter planes used existing airstrips to protect bombers on their way to Japan.

The Joe Rosenthal photograph of the marines planting a flag on the mountaintop is probably the most famous war picture in American history. Today, you can see a monument based on this photograph at the United States Marine Corps War Memorial in Washington, D.C.

Rosa Parks Starts a Boycott

Rosa Parks was among the many African-Americans who struggled for equal rights in the middle decades of the twentieth century. Her refusal to give up her bus seat was followed by her arrest. This sparked the Montgomery, Alabama, bus boycott—led by the young Dr. Martin Luther King, Jr. For more than a year, blacks refused to ride the buses in Montgomery. It was one of the first large-scale protests that helped bring about the passage of the Civil Rights Act of 1964.

Rosa Parks later served for many years as a staff assistant for a United States congressman. You can read more about her life in *Rosa Parks: My Story*.

Ellington and Armstrong—Together at Last

Duke Ellington, born in 1899, and Louis "Satchmo" Armstrong, born in 1901, were two of the most influential jazz musicians of the twentieth century. Ellington was a composer, an arranger, and a pianist, although someone once said, "Duke's real instrument is his orchestra."

Playing the trumpet, Armstrong perfected the jazz solo. At the same time, he sang many popular songs in his rough, distinctive voice. You can hear these two musicians on the only album they made together—*The Great Summit*—done in 1961. Besides "Duke's Place," other Ellington songs they recorded were "I'm Just a Lucky So and So," "Mood Indigo," "In a Mellow Tone," and "It Don't Mean a Thing (If It Ain't Got That Swing)."

Neil Armstrong Steps on the Moon!

On July 20, 1969, two astronauts—Neil Armstrong and Edwin "Buzz" Aldrin—landed and walked on the moon. A third astronaut, Michael Collins, circled the moon in the command ship Columbia, which would take all three men back to Earth. The space explorers brought home with them rock and soil samples and photographs. They also placed an American flag and set up automatic science equipment on the moon.

The moon landing, viewed by millions around the world on television, was the climax of a manned moon-landing program that started in 1961, during the presidency of John F. Kennedy. It involved astronauts, scientists, engineers, and American workers from all walks of life. The entire project, combining scientific theory, technology, and old-fashioned bravery, is one of the most momentous achievements in human history.

We Remember 9/11

On September 11, 2001, nineteen terrorists hijacked four American airliners. Two planes, used as missiles, were flown into the two tallest World Trade Center buildings in New York City, causing both to collapse. Another plane was flown into the Pentagon in Washington, D.C. The fourth plane, due to the bravery of some of the passengers, crashed in Pennsylvania before it could reach its intended target.

In all, around 3,000 people died in what was the most damaging terrorist attack on American soil in the nation's history. Since then, tens of thousands of visitors have come, and are still coming, to the site to pay their respects to those who lost their lives.

For Jeff Roberts and Jackie Schrock, with love and affection
—R. B.

To Mom and Dad
—B. S.

Henry Holt and Company, LLC
Publishers since 1866
115 West 18th Street
New York, New York 10011
www.henryholt.com

Henry Holt is a registered trademark of Henry Holt and Company, LLC
Text copyright © 2004 by Robert Burleigh
Illustrations copyright © 2004 by Bruce Strachan
All rights reserved.
Distributed in Canada by H. B. Fenn and Company Ltd.

Library of Congress Cataloging-in-Publication Data
Burleigh, Robert.
American moments: scenes from American history / Robert Burleigh; illustrated by Bruce Strachan.
p. cm.
Summary: A look at a cross-section of people and events in American history
from 1621 to 2001 representing the many facets of American life.
1. United States—History—Anecdotes—Juvenile literature.
2. United States—Biography—Anecdotes—Juvenile literature.
[1. United States—History—Anecdotes. 2. United States—Biography.]
I. Strachan, Bruce, 1959–, ill. II. Title.
E178.3.B93 2004   973-dc21   2003007067

ISBN 0-8050-7082-6 / First Edition—2004
Printed in the United States of America on acid-free paper.
1 3 5 7 9 10 8 6 4 2

The artist used a mixed media of clay, wood, and oil paint combined
with large-format photography to create the illustrations for this book.